Sparkle Explores the Science of Photography

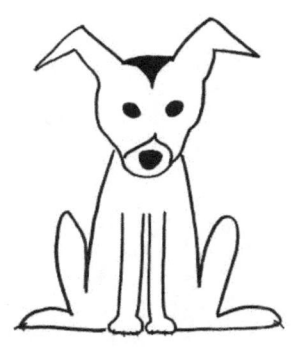 

By Elizabeth Bixby

This book is dedicated to the Peoria Riverfront Museum and the wonders of art and science they share with our community.

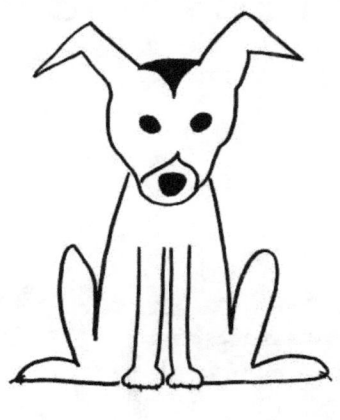

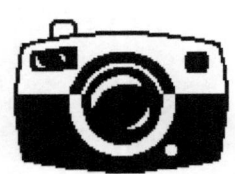

Hi! I'm Sparkle!

I love art and science.
That's why I enjoy
photography so much
because it's both!

Photography uses science to create art.

Photography requires a camera to take the photo.

A camera captures images and records that moment to film or a digital reader card.

It seems like magic.

Actually, light reflects off objects and people to form an image for the camera. The light creates the magic.

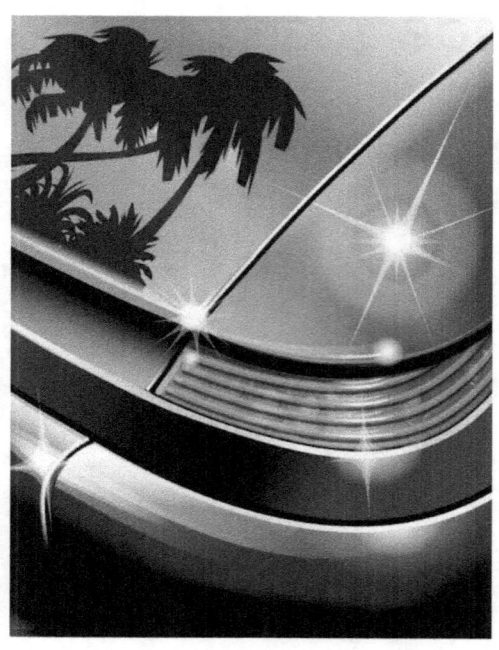

Even the light from a camera flash can perform wonder as they stop motion in a photo.

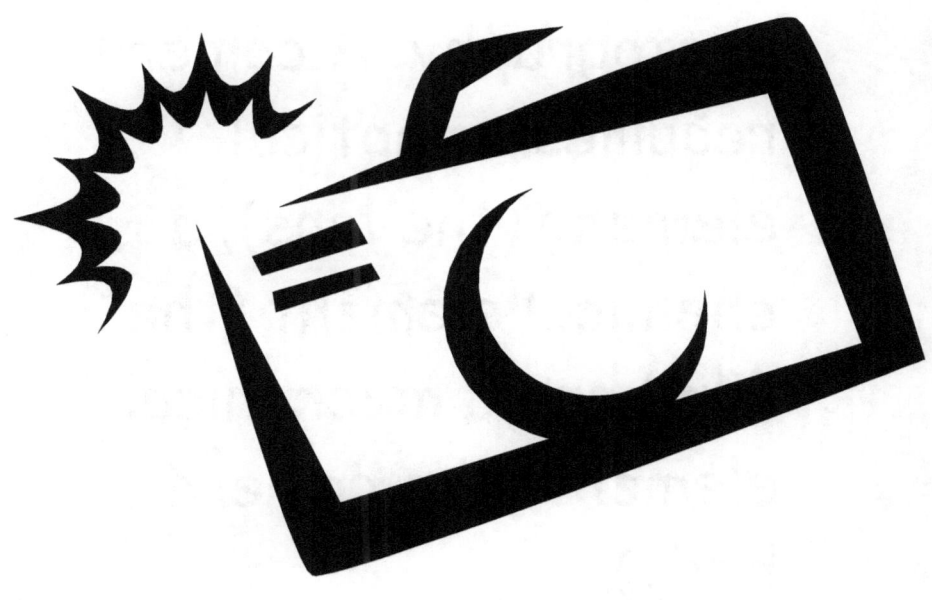

Let's learn how this magic works.

Three basic elements combine to create the technology of photography. A camera requires an optical element (the lens), a chemical element (the film) and a mechanical element (the camera body).

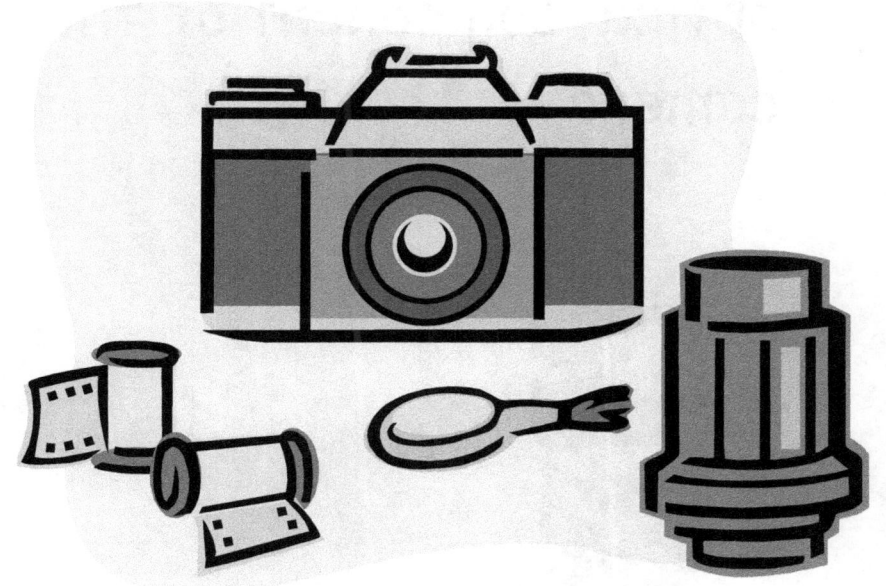

The lens makes the optical component of the camera.

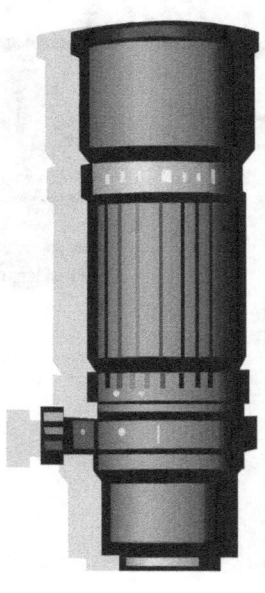

Optic means seeing so the lens sees the subject.

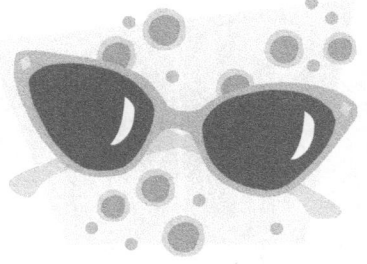

At its simplest, a lens can be as simple as a curved piece of glass or plastic.

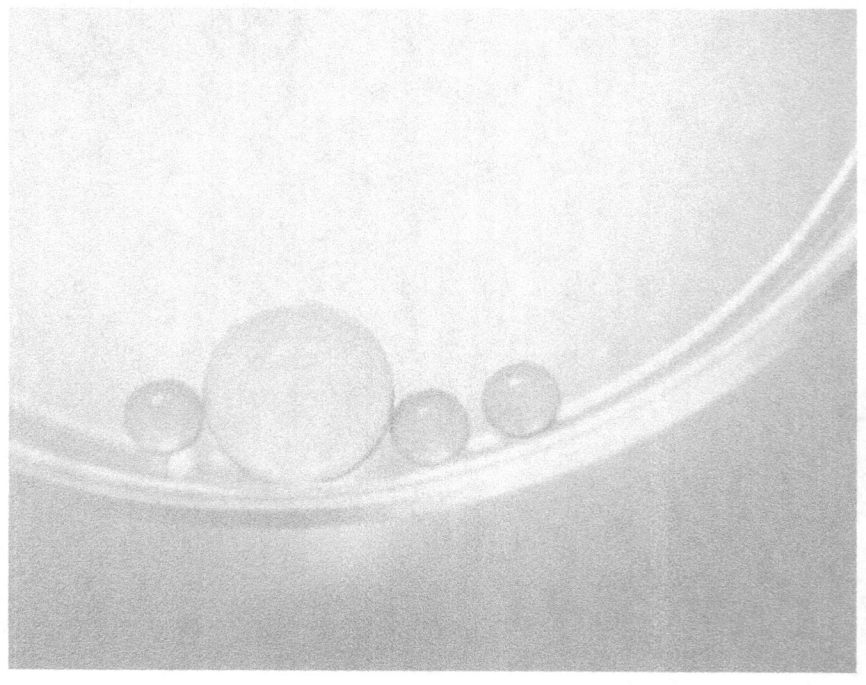

It takes beams of light reflecting off of an object and redirects them together to form an image that looks just like the scene in front of the lens.

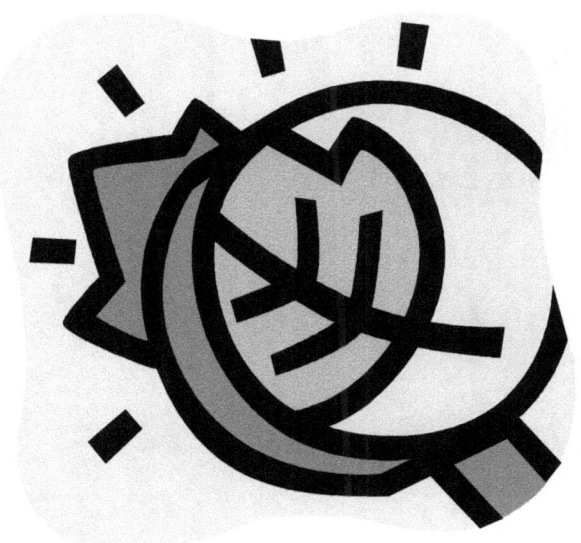

Wow!

How can a piece of glass do this?

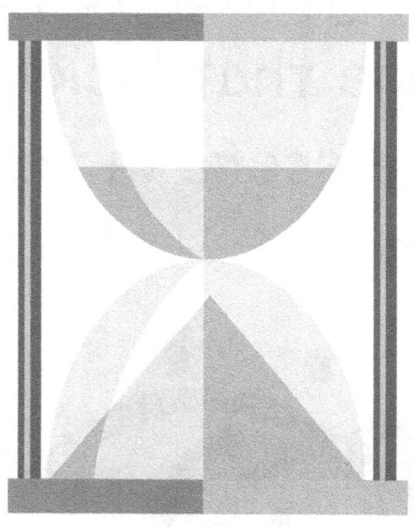

When the light bounces off of one subject to another, it changes speed.

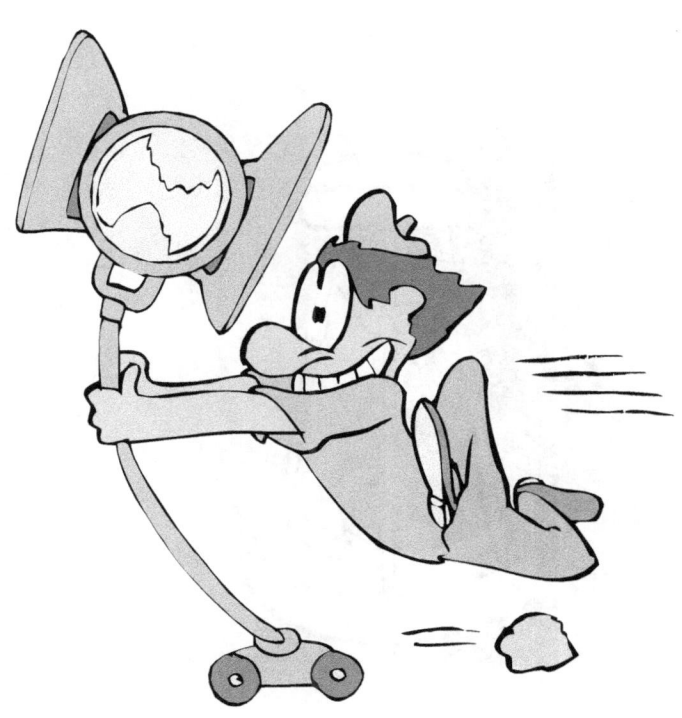

Light travels faster through the air than it can pass through glass, so a lens slows it down.

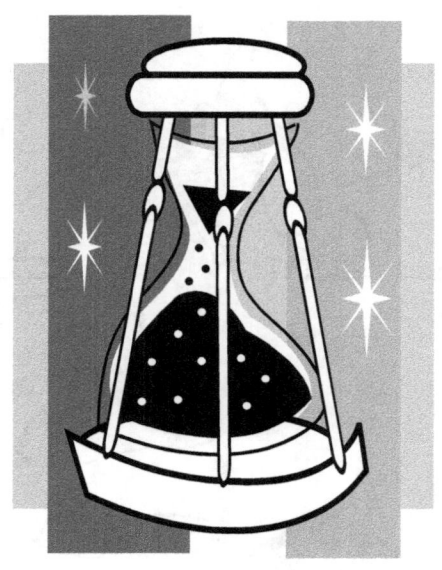

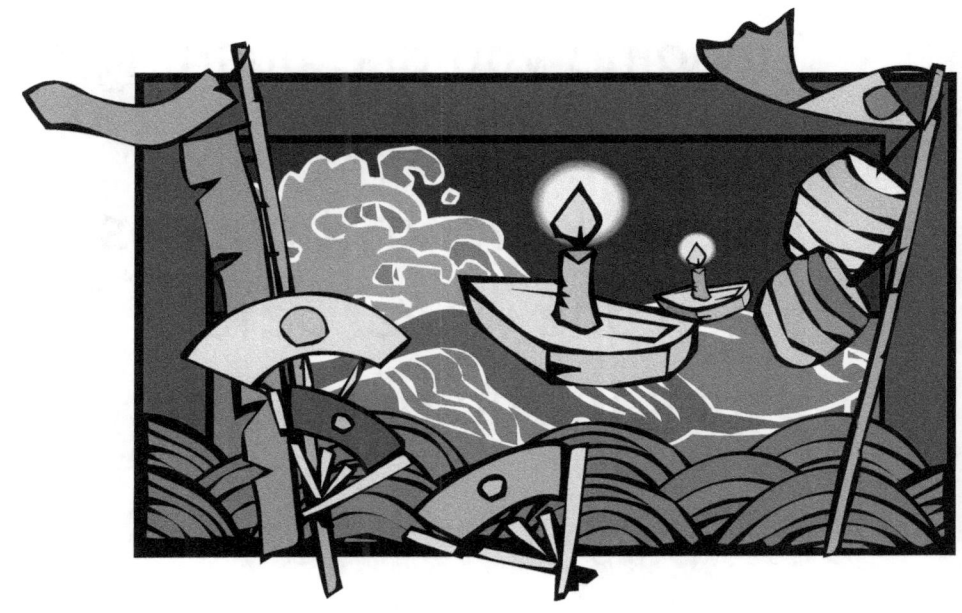

When light waves enter a piece of glass from the angles, different parts of the wave reach the glass at different times.

Imagine you are pushing a baby carriage down a sidewalk. What happens when one wheel gets stuck in the grass?

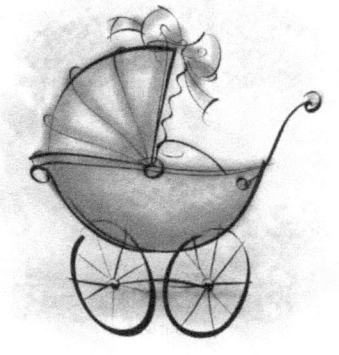

It turns, doesn't it? Because the left wheel moves faster than the other wheel, the carriage turns as it moves onto the grass.

The same effect happens when light rays enter the glass of the lens at an angle. It turns in one direction. It bends again when it leaves the glass because parts of the light wave enter the air and speed up before other parts of the wave.

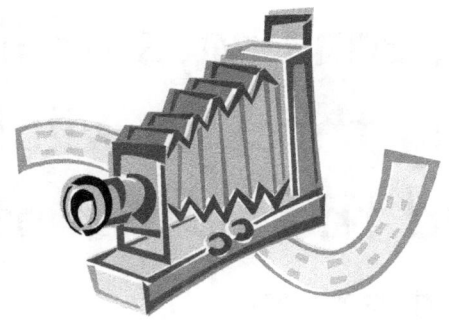

In a standard convex lens, one or both sides of the glass curves out.

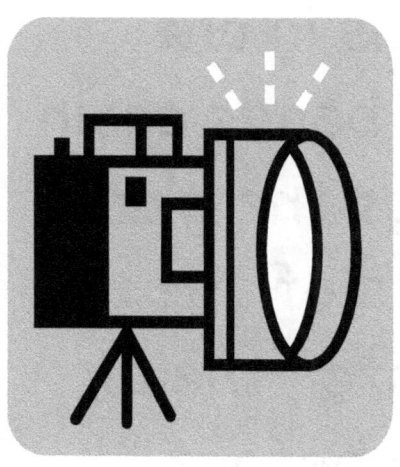

This means rays of light passing through will bend toward the center of the lens on entry.

In a double convex lens, like a magnifying glass, the light bends when it exits as well as when it enters.

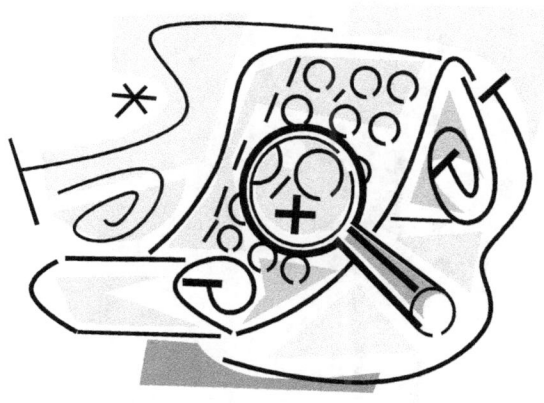

This effectively reverses the path of light from an object.

Visualize a light source -
- say a candle - as it
sends out light in all
directions.

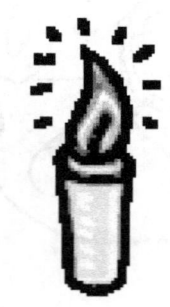

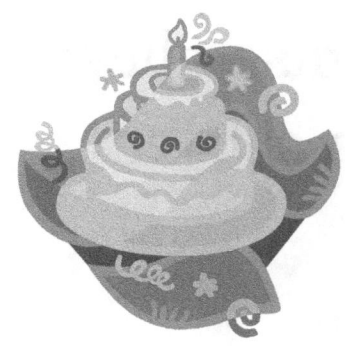

The rays of light all start at the same point, the candle's flame. A converging lens takes those rays and redirects them back to one point.

At the point where the rays come together, you get a real image of the candle.

A camera lens also allows
you to view the subject.

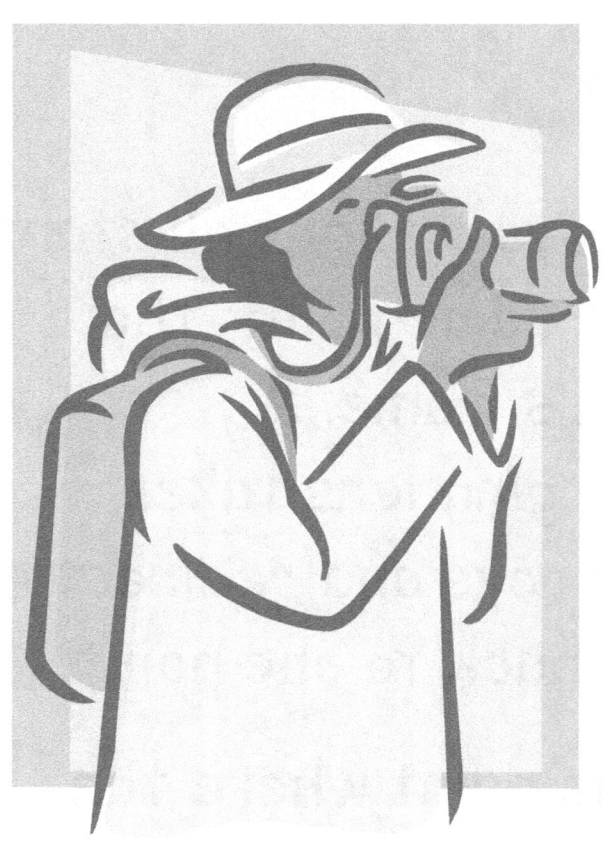

When the camera button is pushed, the lens briefly opens and records light which makes the photograph.

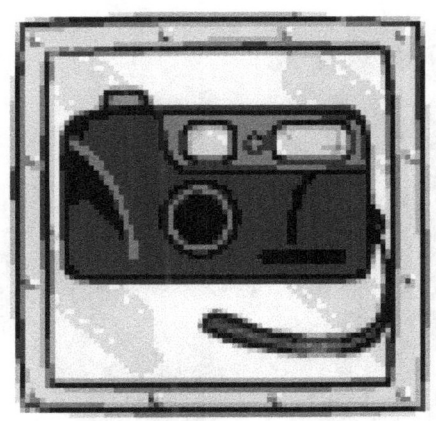

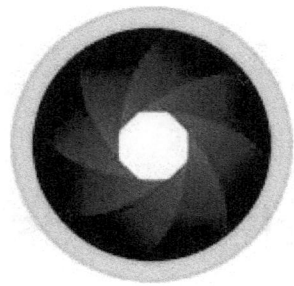

The lens opening inside the lens body is called the aperture.

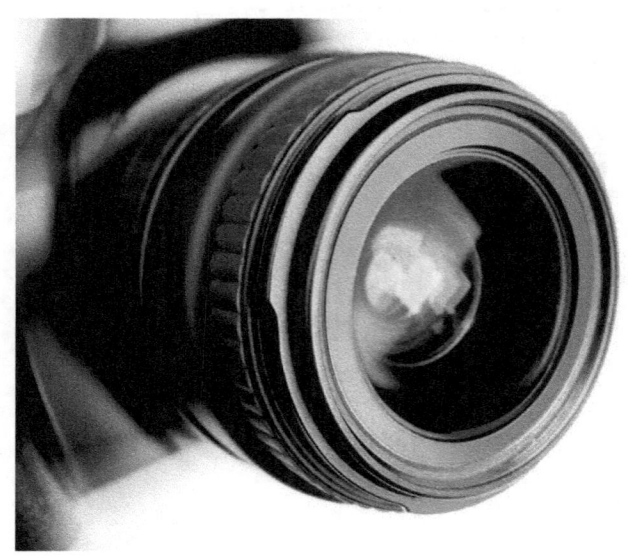

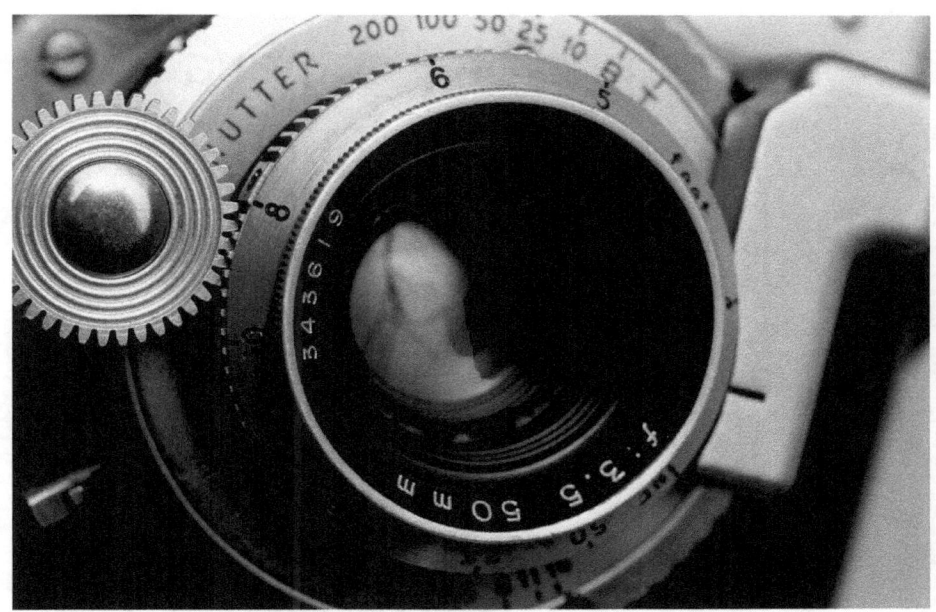

The amount of time the
lens stays open is called
the shutter speed.

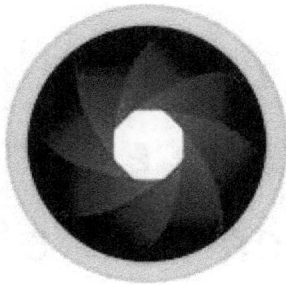

Imagine the camera as a
water faucet and the
photo you want to make
is an empty cup.

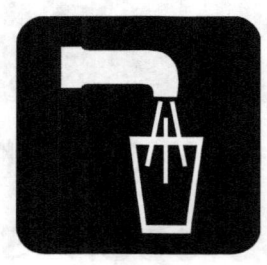

You need the right size
faucet and the perfect
amount of time to fill the
cup to the perfect spot.

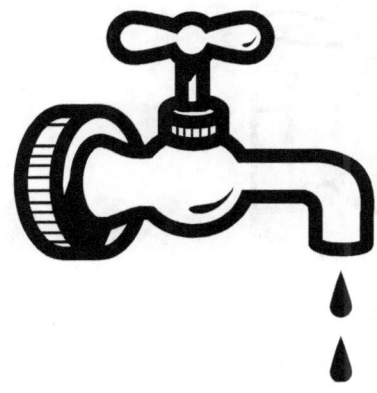

So the camera aperture would be the size of the faucet.

If the faucet opening is very small, it will take longer to fill a cup.
Right?

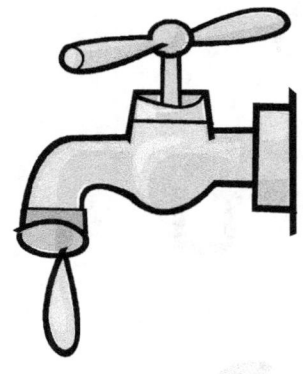

Then, the opposite would mean that if the faucet opening was huge, it would only take a split second to fill a cup.

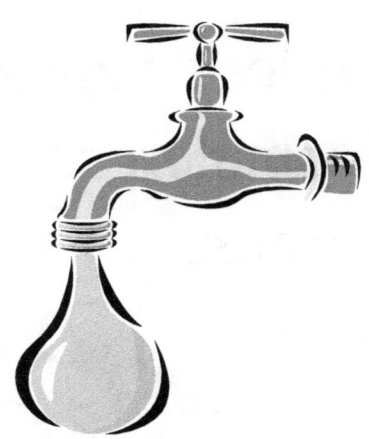

The aperture, the size of the lens opening is usually known as the f/stop number. The number is figured out by the ratio of the length of the lens to the size of the aperture hole size.

A lens typically has a common set of marked f-stops.

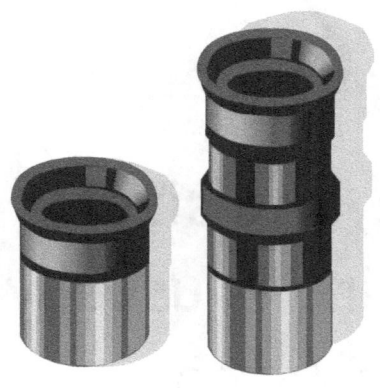

A lower f-number means a larger aperture opening which allows more light to reach the film or image sensor.

The higher the f/stop number, the clearer the photo. If the aperture is small, it has to be open a long time, right? That long time allows the details of the photo to be sharp. Photographers need tripods for long exposures.

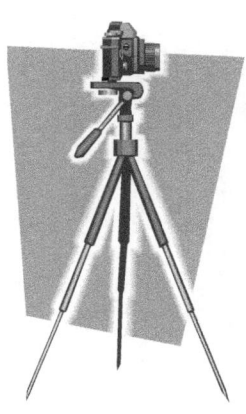

If you use a small aperture, like an f/4, not everything will be in focus because the lens will not be open long enough to include all of the details.

This is called a shallow depth of field.

Have you ever seen a photo when only one thing is sharp and everything else is blurred? That's a shallow depth of field all right.

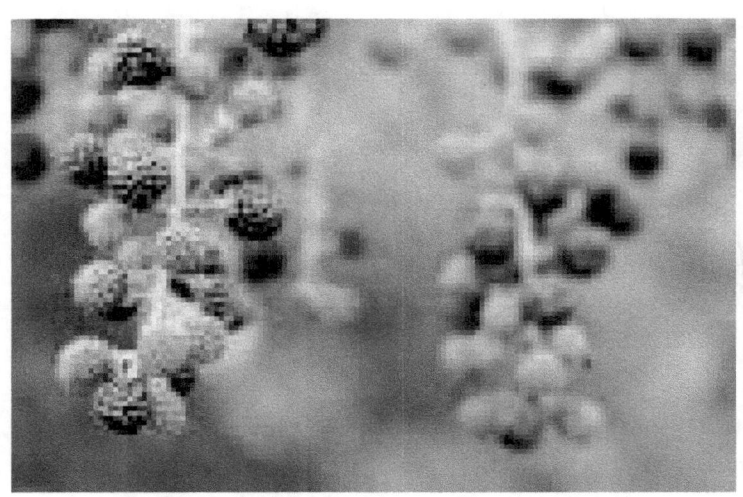

Longer lenses pass less light due to the greater distance the light has to travel; shorter lenses (a shorter focal length) will be brighter with the same size of aperture.

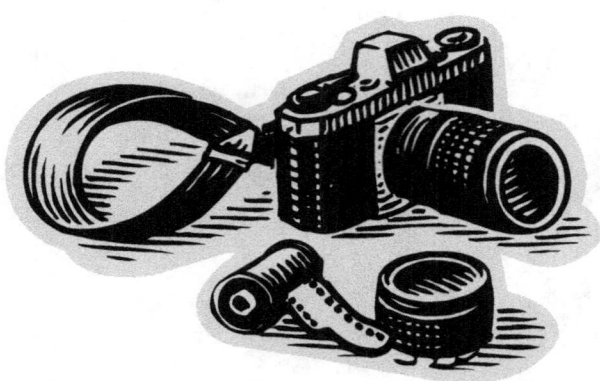

Many cameras adjust most or all of these controls automatically.

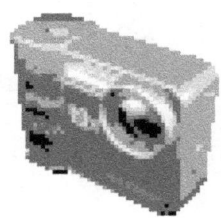

True photographers understand how to work the control to make the photo look like they want it to look.

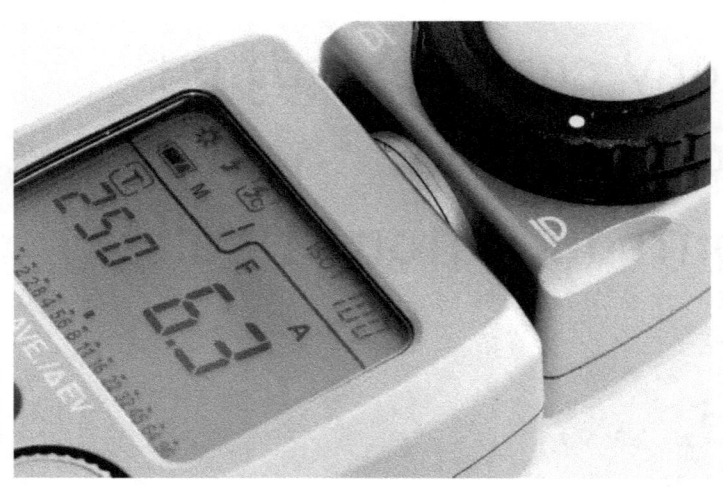

Therefore, photographers use the f/stops to control the lens to expose the film or to the RAW file in digital cameras.

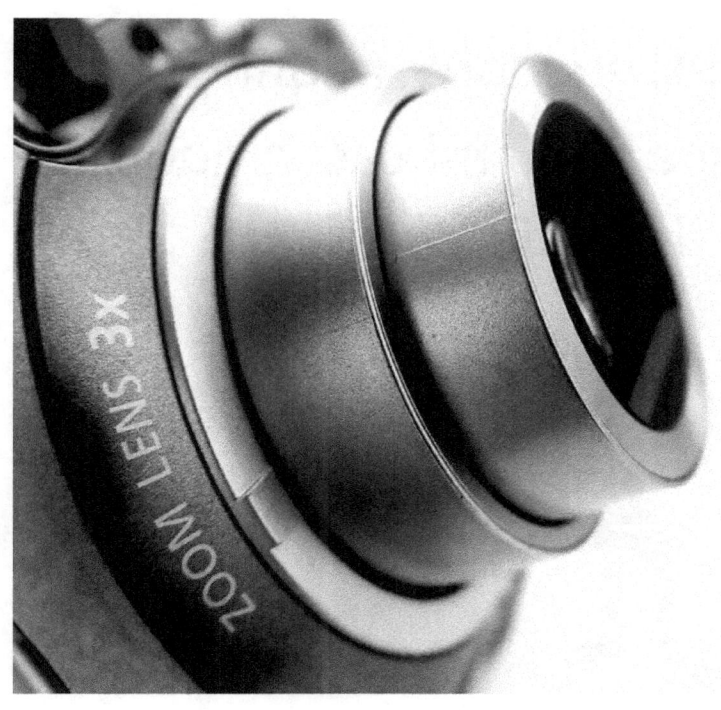

This leads to the second component which is the chemicals. Whether briefly stored and then printed or with film and then printing, photography requires a carefully mixed amounts of chemicals.

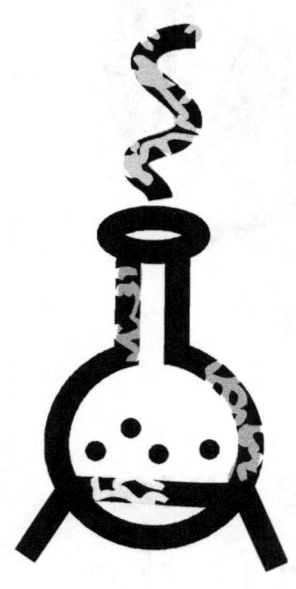

Today, photography labs and ink cartridges primarily control the chemicals, although they are a main component of photography.

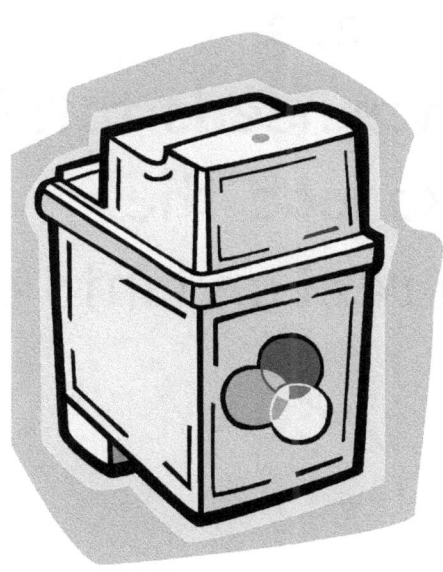

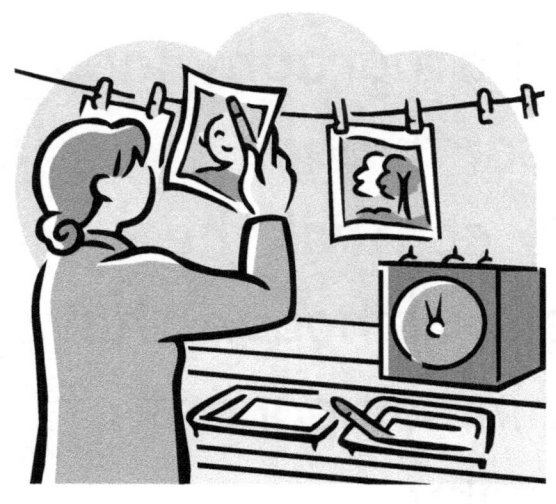

In a darkroom, a photographer needs total blackness to load the film onto a reel and into a tank.

Then for a certain amount of calculated time, a chemical developer poured into the steel tank develops the film and turns the light exposed part of the film to silver halides.

Then the developed is poured put and a stop bath stops the developing process. After thirty seconds of aggitation, shaking the tank, the stop bath goes out and a fixer goes into the tank for a limited amount of time as well to fix the image to the film.

After the film is fixed and the exposed silver is washed away and set on the negative, it comes out of the tank after a water wash.

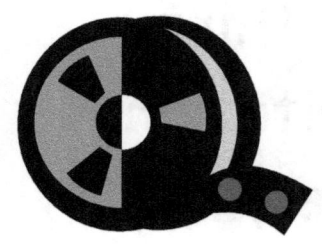

The film needs to dry completely before making prints.

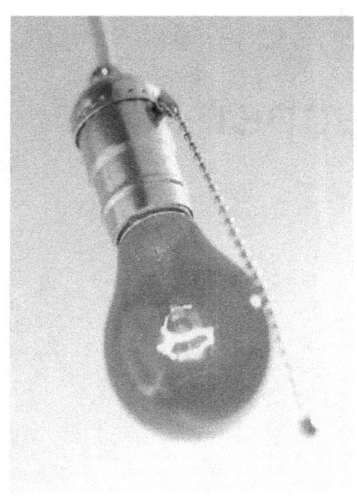

A red light can be used when making photos. The negative of film goes through the lens slide of the enlarger.

For a special amount of time, light shines from the enlarger through the negative onto the photographic paper.

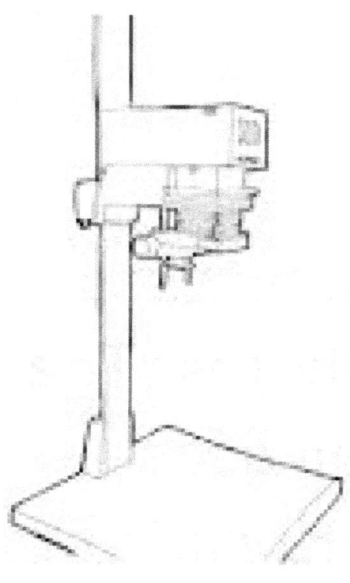

A photographer uses tests strips to determine the correct exposure for the photographer. Then for a certain amount of time, an enlarger light shines through the film onto the paper making a latent or invisible image. Then the paper goes into a tray of developer, stop bath, fixer and the water wash and hung on a lie to dry.

The darkroom reminds me of the camera itself because camera means dark room or chamber.

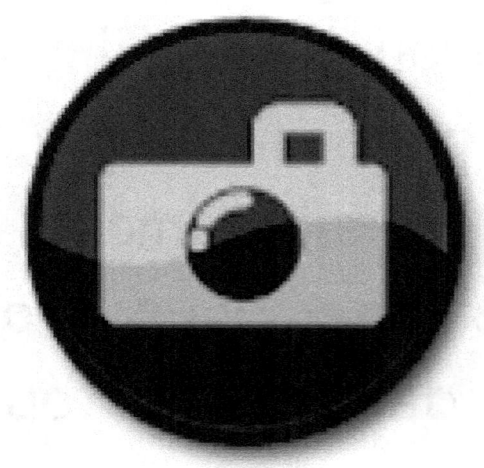

Cameras can range from small to very large, a whole room kept dark while the object to be photographed in another room is properly lighted.

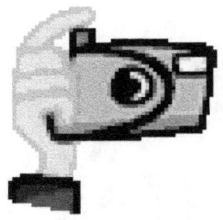

An old saying said the smaller the camera the brighter the photo.

In almost every camera, obtaining a usable exposure must involve, either manually or automatically, a few controls to ensure the photograph is clear, sharp and well lighted.

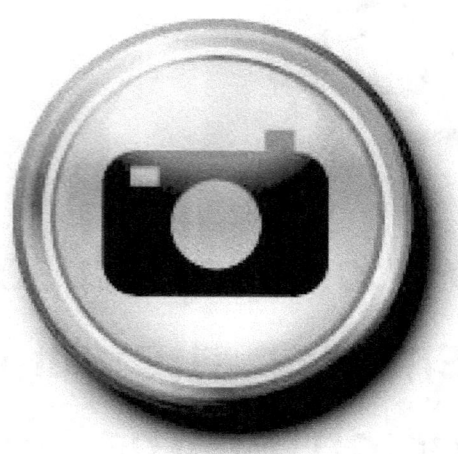

Photography is undoubtedly one of the most important inventions in history -- it has truly transformed how people think of the world.

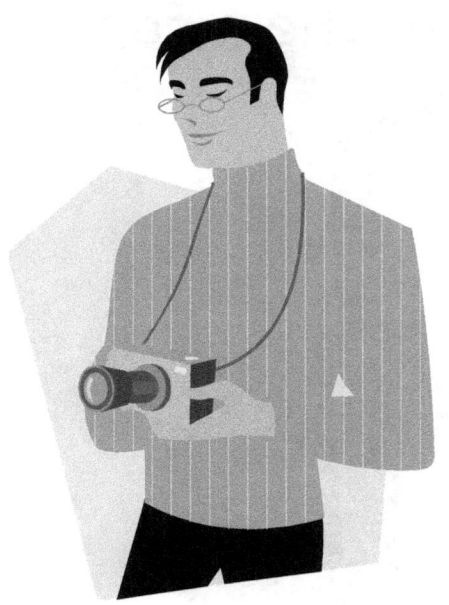

Now we can "see" all sorts of things that are actually many miles -- and years -- from us. Photography lets us capture moments in time and preserve them for years to come.

Rather than me select a project, why don't you take some photos with a camera and experiment with depth of field. You can make your own album with its own theme, for example, your garden or your family. Have fun!

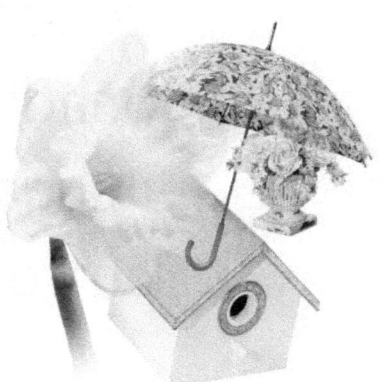

Glossary:

Focus
The position of a viewed object or the adjustment of an optical device necessary to produce a clear image: in focus; out of focus.

Aperture Adjustment of the lens opening, measured as an f/stop number, which controls the amount of light passing through the lens, and in turn the depth of field and the amount of detail in focus.

Aperture also has an effect on depth of field- the higher the f-number, the smaller the opening, the less light, the greater the depth of field, and the more the diffraction blur. The focal length divided by the f-number gives the effective aperture diameter.

Shutter speed	Adjustment of the speed of the shutter to control the amount of time

during which
the imaging
medium is
exposed to
light for each
exposure.
Shutter speed
may be used to
control the
amount of light
striking the
image plane;
'faster'
shutter speeds

(that is, those of shorter duration) decrease both the amount of light and the amount of image blurring from motion of the subject and/or camera.

White Balance

On digital cameras, electronic compensation for the color temperature associated with a given set of lighting conditions, ensuring that white light is registered as such on the imaging chip and therefore that the colors in the frame will appear natural. photographers may use white balance to a blue object in order to obtain a warm color temperature.

Metering

Measurement of exposure so that highlights and shadows are exposed according to the photographer's wishes. Many modern cameras meter and set exposure automatically.

Before automatic exposure, correct exposure was accomplished with the use of a separate light meter or by the photographer's knowledge and experience of gauging correct settings. To translate the amount of light into a usable aperture and shutter speed, the meter needs to adjust for the sensitivity of the film or sensor to light. This is done by setting the "film speed" or ISO sensitivity into the meter.

ISO Speed	Traditionally used to "tell the camera" the film speed of the selected film on film cameras, ISO

speeds are employed on modern digital cameras as an indication of the systems gain from light to numerical output and to control the automatic exposure system. The higher the ISO number the greater the film sensitivity to light, whereas with a lower ISO number, the film is less sensitive to light. A correct combination of ISO speed, aperture, and shutter speed leads to an image that is neither too dark nor too light, hence it is 'correctly exposed', indicated by a centered meter.

Auto focus

On some cameras, the selection of a point in the imaging frame upon which the auto-focus system will attempt to focus. Many cameras feature multiple auto-focus points in the viewfinder.